Prayers for Children at Christmas Time

Children's Christian Prayer Books

BABY PROFESSOR
EDUCATION KIDS

Speedy Publishing LLC
40 E. Main St. #1156
Newark, DE 19711
www.speedypublishing.com

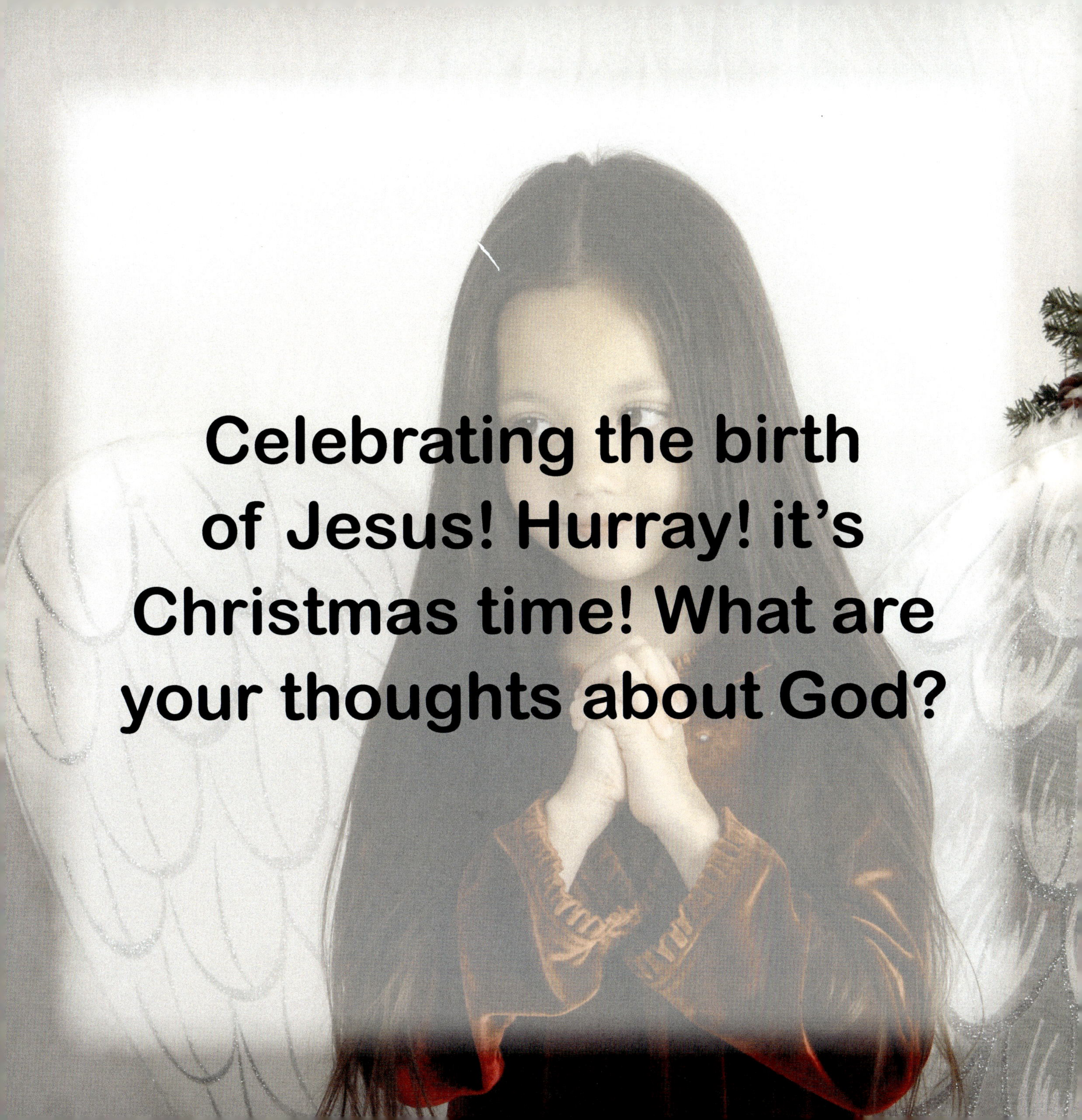

Celebrating the birth of Jesus! Hurray! it's Christmas time! What are your thoughts about God?

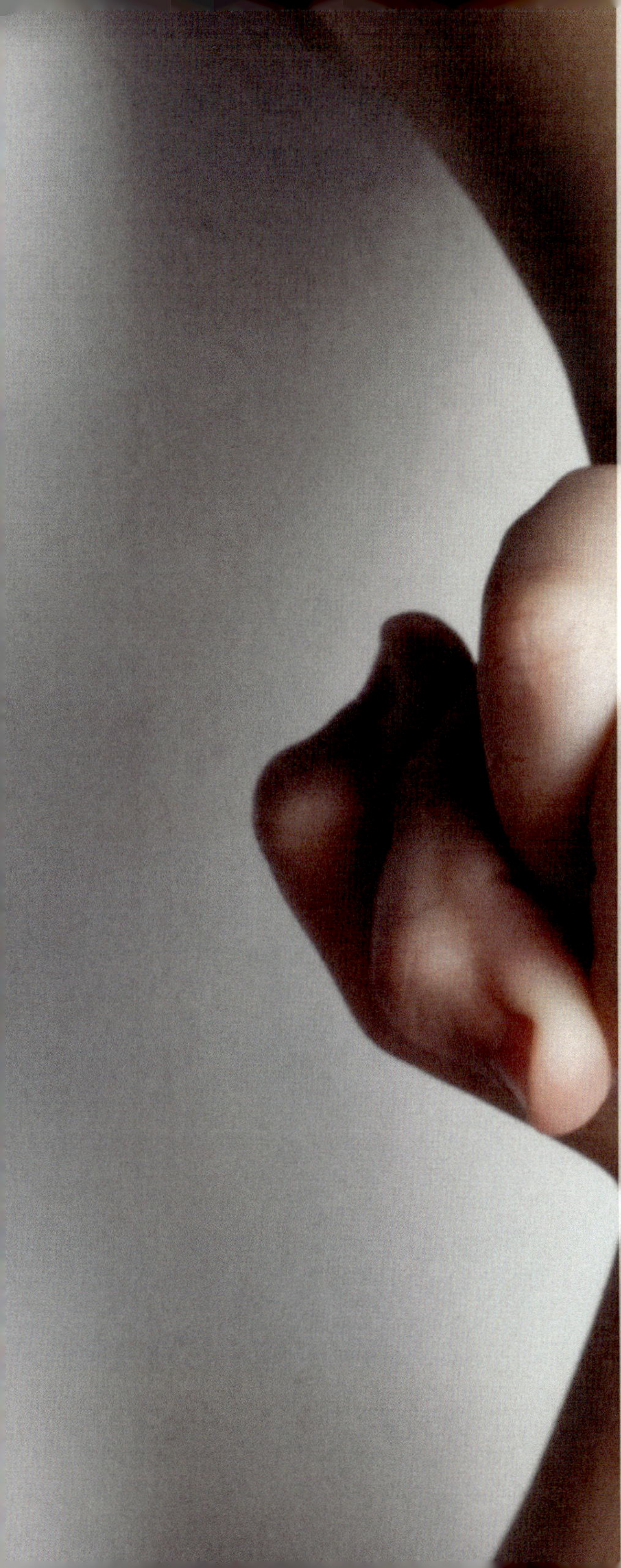

Children of God, this book will teach you prayers for Christmas time. What do you wish to have for Christmas? What do you pray for? Talk every day with Jesus through these prayers, or in your own words, and you will be closer to him and more caring for all the people in the world.

Christmas is a big celebration for all Christians around the world. They are celebrating the birth of Jesus. Christians in most countries display their traditional Christmas decoration such as lanterns, mistletoe and Christmas trees. People around the world observe the spirit of Christmas recognizing it as the best time of the year. The sparkling lights in windows and on the walls delight the soul.

What do you ask God at Christmas time? Here are some prayers for the season.

A Prayer for Christmas

Jesus, we adore you.
You are the Light of
the World,
As we celebrate your
birthday, teach us
to be humble and
to be forgiving.

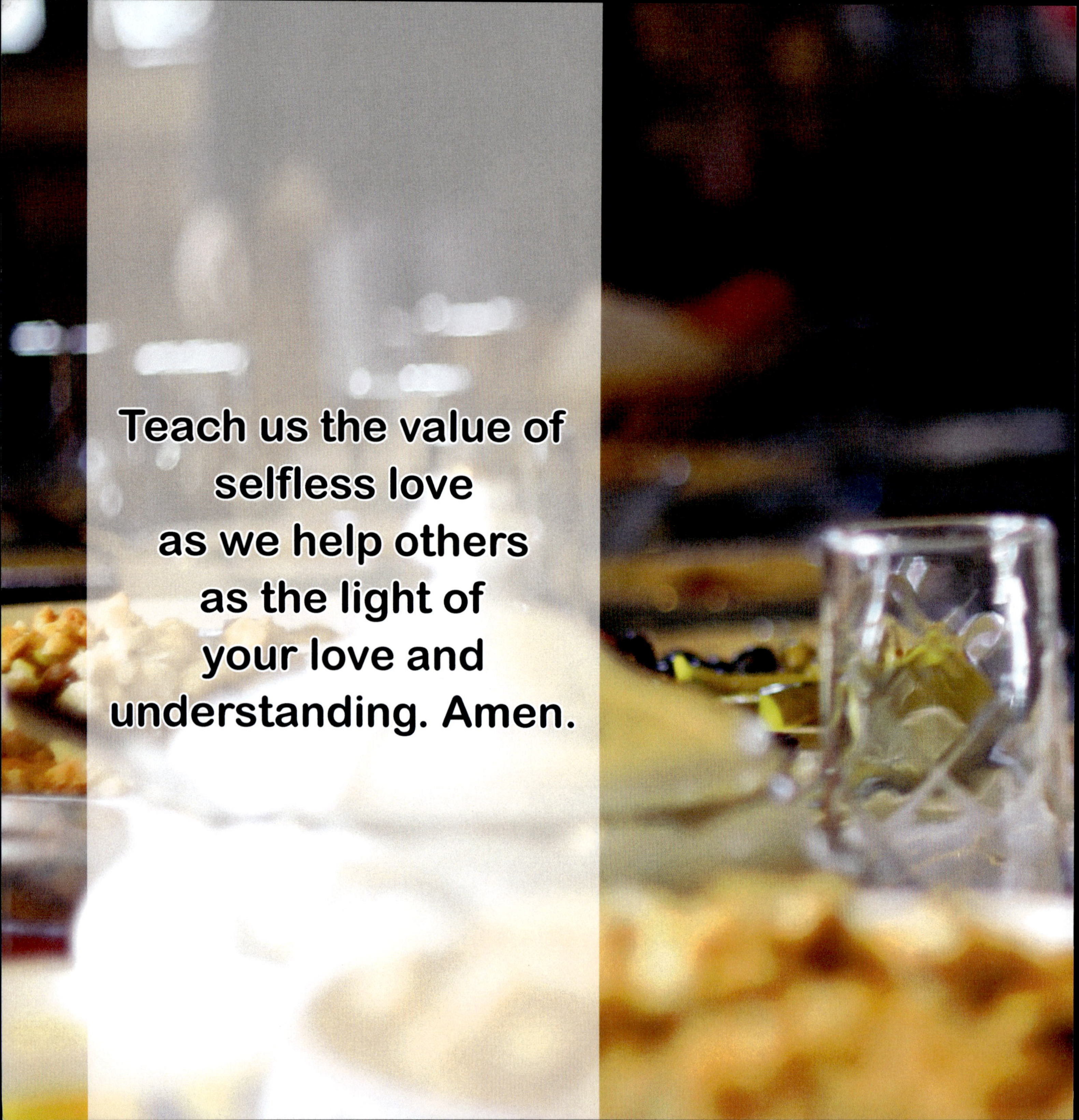

Teach us the value of
selfless love
as we help others
as the light of
your love and
understanding. Amen.

A Christmas Celebration

Baby Jesus you
inspire our hearts
to love and to
rejoice.
We love you with
all our hearts
and minds.

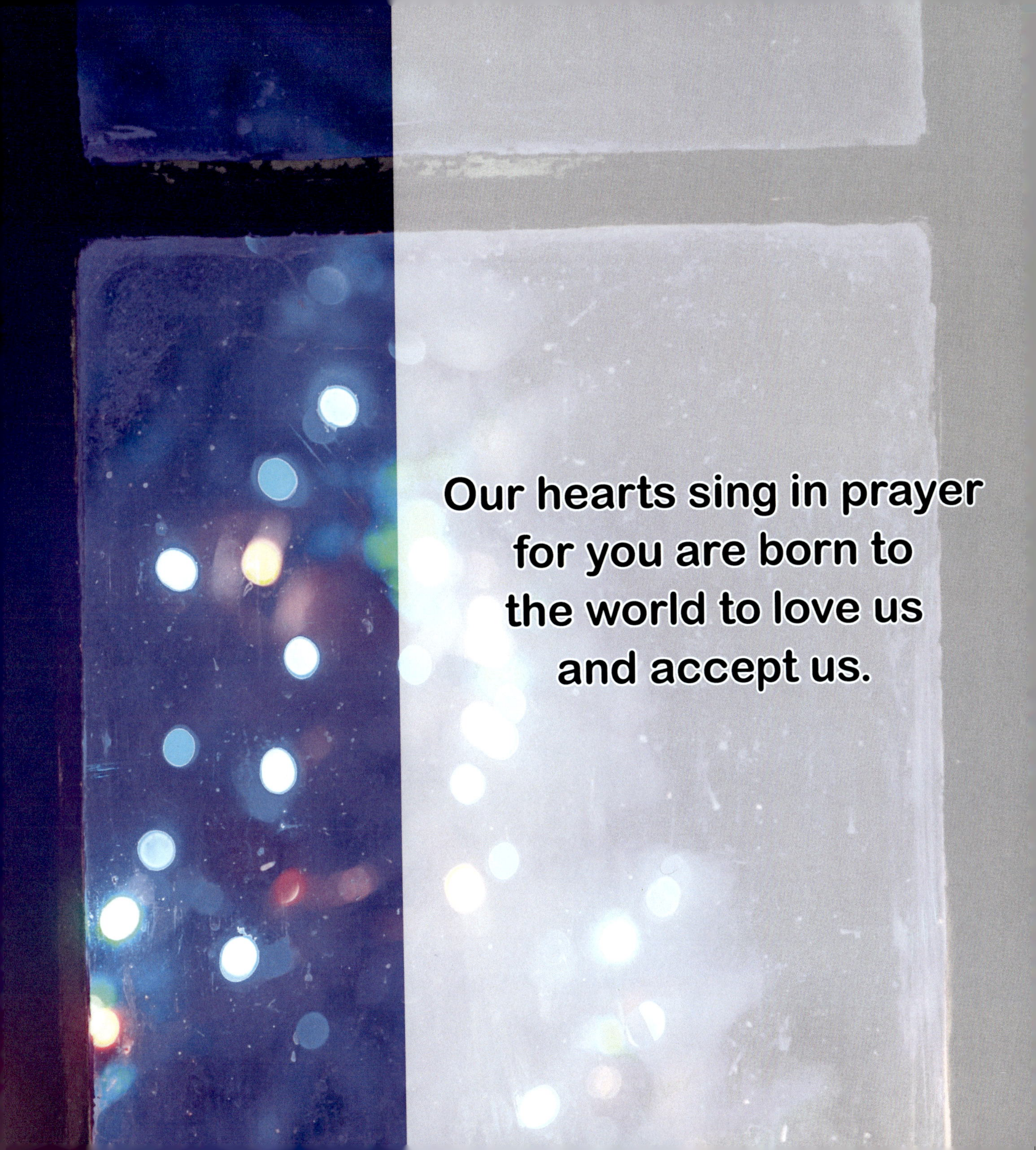

Our hearts sing in prayer
for you are born to
the world to love us
and accept us.

We love you Jesus.
Your sacrifice
means a lot.
Your birthday is a
reason to rejoice.

On Christmas day we
come to worship you.
We thank Mother Mary
for loving us too!

Christmas, Time to Rejoice

We are the faithful,
therefore we
celebrate,
Baby Jesus is with us
today!
A big celebration
indeed

For the love of God
comes to us,
the baby in the
manger is the savior
of the world!
Behold! Prepare your
gifts of thanksgiving.

The Precious little
Baby, the King of all!
Come and worship Him
Christmas is here,
Baby Jesus is here!

With love and hope, we
celebrate.
We share the love as
we sing and pray!
Praise the Lord,
Jesus is with us!

Together we greet him
on this special day,
with faith and
devotion. Amen!

There are more prayers for children at Christmas time. Research and have fun!

35595940R00024

Made in the USA
Columbia, SC
21 November 2018